THIS WALKER BOOK BELONGS TO:

_____

_____

_____

_____

First published 1994
by Walker Books Ltd, 87 Vauxhall Walk
London SE11 5HJ

This edition published 2001

10 9 8 7 6 5 4 3 2 1

Text © 1994 Foxbusters Ltd
Illustrations © 1994 Anita Jeram

The right of Dick King-Smith to be identified as author
of this work has been asserted by him in accordance
with the Copyright, Designs and Patents Act 1988

This book has been typeset in Baskerville

Printed in Hong Kong

British Library Cataloguing in Publication Data:
a catalogue record for this book
is available from the British Library

ISBN 0-7445-6278-3

# I LOVE GUINEA-PIGS

Dick King-Smith

illustrated by

Anita Jeram

WALKER BOOKS
AND SUBSIDIARIES
LONDON • BOSTON • SYDNEY

There's a silly old saying that
if you hold a guinea-pig up
by its tail, its eyes
will drop out.

Well of course they wouldn't,

even if you could. Which you couldn't,

because guinea-pigs don't have tails.

What do guinea-pigs have in common with pigs?

The males and females are known as "boars" and "sows".

And they aren't pigs either. They're rodents – like mice and rats and squirrels.

Rodents have special front teeth which are brilliant for gnawing things. These teeth go on growing throughout the animal's life, and are self-sharpening.

As for the other bit of their name, guinea-pigs were first brought to Europe about four hundred years ago by Spanish sailors, probably from a country in South America called Dutch Guiana. And the sailors called them "guiana pigs".

In fact the guinea-pig is a member
of the cavy family, and its
Latin name is *Cavia porcellus*
(which means a piggy-looking cavy).

Anyway, whatever they're called,
it's the way they look that I've
always liked. They're so
chunky and chubby
and cuddly, with their blunt
heads and sturdy bodies and short legs.

Smooth

Peruvian

They come in loads of different colours, and
they can be smooth-coated or rough-coated
or long-coated, not to mention
the other varieties.
I've kept hundreds of
guinea-pigs over the last fifty years,
but I've always liked the Abyssinians best.

Crested

Sheltie

Abyssinians

Guinea-pigs are such sensible animals.

They're awfully easy to keep,

because they aren't fussy.

They don't like the cold, of course, or the damp, any more  than you would, and they're not happy living in a poky little place, any more than you would be. But as long as they have a comfortable warm dry place to live, guinea-pigs are as happy as Larry.

Guinea-pigs like a really big roomy hutch, or, better still, a wire run out on the grass.

13

They're hardy animals, and don't often fall ill. Properly looked after, they can live a long time.

Most guinea-pigs live for around five to eight years.

I once had a Crested sow
called Zen. She lived two years
with me and then eight more
with one of my daughters.
People's hair grows whiter
as they age, but Zen's
grew darker.

Guinea-pigs need plenty of food.

They love eating, just like you do, and feeding

them is half the fun of keeping them.

Some people, of course, feed them

nothing but hay and pellets from

the pet shop and they're quite all

right. But how boring a diet like that must

be, both for the piggy-looking

cavy and its

owner.

I always used to give my
guinea-pigs lots of other kinds

of food as well: cabbage and cauliflower leaves,
carrots, bits of bread and apple peelings, and
wild plants like dandelion
and clover. I gave them
water, too, of course.

Guinea-pigs need
clean drinking
water every day. And their water
bottle often needs washing,
because they like blowing bits
of food back up the spout.

One especially nice thing
about guinea-pigs is that
if you handle them
regularly, and carry them about, stroke
them, talk to them, and make a fuss
of them, they become really
fond of you.

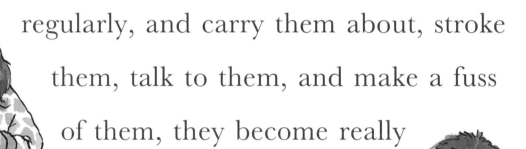

The proper way to pick up
a guinea-pig is with one hand
over its shoulders and the other
supporting its bottom.

19

Another nice thing about guinea-pigs is that they talk a lot.

When they want food or water, they often give a sort of whistle, sometimes low, sometimes loud.

Boars say CHUTTER when they're squaring up for a fight.

So do sows when their babies pester them too much.

Other things guinea-pigs say are

PUTT
CHUT
TWEET
and DRR.

But when one guinea-pig says PURR to another

guinea-pig, it's as plain as the nose on your face

that it only means one thing:

"I love you."

And that brings me on
to what's best of all about
keeping guinea-pigs – baby ones.
Because their ancestors, the wild cavies
of South America, lived out in the
open with enemies all about them,
their young ones had to be
ready to run for it.

So the guinea-pig sow carries
her unborn litter for a very
long time, about seventy days,

and they arrive in
the world fully furred, with their
eyes open and their mouths already

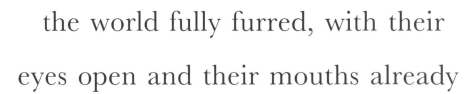

filled with teeth.
Newborn guinea-pigs
are such a comical sight.
Their heads and feet look too big for their bodies.

Baby rabbits are born blind and naked and helpless, but not baby guinea-pigs.

But almost immediately
they show an interest in those two
favourite guinea-pig pursuits –

 eating

and conversation.

Of all the guinea-pigs I've kept, there were two that I shall never forget. Both were Abyssinians, both were boars, and each in his time fathered dozens of lovely big-headed, big-footed babies.

One was a bright golden colour,
and his name was King Arthur.
The other was a blue roan called
Beach Boy. Both are buried in
my garden.

There's a solitary apple tree at the edge
of my lawn, and I like to look at it and think
that under it Beach Boy and King Arthur
lie peacefully, one on one side of the tree,
one on the other.

I'm not sad about this –
just happy to remember
what a lot of pleasure
I've had from all
my guinea-pigs.

# INDEX

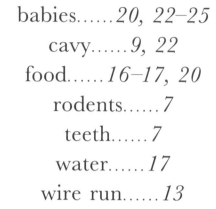

Look up the pages to find out
about all these guinea-pig things.
Don't forget to look at both kinds
of words: this kind and **this kind.**

## A note from the author

Dick King-Smith says he has "always had
a soft spot for guinea-pigs. I started
keeping them when I was six and only stopped,
with great regret, when I was sixty."

## A note from the illustrator

Anita Jeram also illustrated Dick King-Smith's
**All Pigs are Beautiful**, and notes,
"One of the things pigs and guinea-pigs have
in common is their love for food."
Anita's own guinea-pig is
named Hungry Hank.

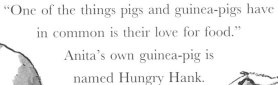

# NOTES FOR TEACHERS

The READ AND WONDER series is an innovative and versatile resource for reading, thinking and discovery. Each book invites children to become excited about a topic, see how varied information books can be, and want to find out more.

**Reading aloud** The story form makes these books ideal for reading aloud – in their own right or as part of a cross-curricular topic, to a child or to a whole class. After you've introduced children to the books in this way, they can revisit and enjoy them again and again.

**Shared reading** Big Book editions are available for several titles, so children can read along, discuss the topic, and comment on the different ways information is presented – to wonder together.

**Group and guided reading** Children need to experience a range of reading materials. Information books like these help develop the skills of reading to learn, as part of learning to read. With the support of a reading group, children can become confident, flexible readers.

**Paired reading** It's fun to take turns to read the information in the main text or in the captions. With a partner, children can explore the pages to satisfy their curiosity and build their understanding.

**Individual reading** These books can be read for interest and pleasure by children at home and in school.

**Research** Once children have been introduced to these books through reading aloud, they can use them for independent or group research, as part of a curricular topic.

**Children's own writing** You can offer these books as strong models for children's own information writing. They can record their observations and findings about a topic, make field notes and sketches, and add extra snippets of information for the reader.

Above all, Read and Wonders are to be enjoyed, and encourage children to develop a lasting curiosity about the world they live in.

*Sue Ellis, Centre for Language in Primary Education*